FPL
J 641.59

Perma
$16.95

P9-CDS-969
3 1213 00773 6194

DISCARD

FRAMINGHAM PUBLIC LIBRARY
APR 0 5 2001

Exploring History through Simple Recipes

California Gold Rush Cooking

by Lisa Golden Schroeder

Consultant: Joseph R. Conlin, Author of
Bacon, Beans, and Galantines:
Food and Foodways on the Western Mining Frontier

Blue Earth Books

an imprint of Capstone Press
Mankato, Minnesota

Blue Earth Books are published by Capstone Press
151 Good Counsel Drive, P.O. Box 669, Mankato, Minnesota 56002
http://www.capstone-press.com

Copyright © 2001 Capstone Press. All rights reserved.
No part of this book may be reproduced without written permission from the publisher.
The publisher takes no responsibility for the use of any of the materials
or methods described in this book, nor for the products thereof.
Printed in the United States of America.

Library of Congress Cataloging-in-Publication Data
Schroeder, Lisa Golden.
    California Gold Rush cooking / by Lisa Golden Schroeder.
    p. cm.—(Exploring history through simple recipes)
    Includes bibliographical references and index.
    Summary: Discusses the everyday life, cooking methods, common foods, and hardships and celebrations during the Gold Rush in California.
Includes recipes.
    ISBN 0-7368-0603-2
    1. Cookery, American—California style—Juvenile literature. 2. California—Gold discoveries—History—Juvenile literature. [1. California—Gold discoveries. 2. Cookery, American.] I. Title. II. Series.
TX715.2.C34 S37 2001
641.59794—dc21   00-036767
                                                                                                              CIP

Editorial credits
Editors: Rachel Koestler and Kay M. Olson
Designer: Heather Kindseth
Illustrator: Linda Clavel
Photo researcher: Katy Kudela

Photo credits
FPG International LLC, cover; North Wind Picture Archives, 6, 8, 10, 12, 15; Archive photos, 7; Gregg Andersen, cover (background), 11, 17, 20, 23, 29; California State Library, 13, 16-17, 24, 28-29; Library of Congress, 14; New York Historical Society, 19; The Huntington Library, Idaho State Historical Society, 22; Sharlot Hall Museum, 26; University of Idaho Library, 25

Acknowledgments
Blue Earth Books thanks JoAnn Levy, author of *They Saw the Elephant: Women in the California Gold Rush,* for her assistance with this book.

Editor's note
Adult supervision may be needed for some recipes in this book. All recipes have been tested. Although based on historical foods, recipes have been modernized and simplified for today's young cooks.

1 2 3 4 5 6 06 05 04 03 02 01

Contents

Cooking Help

Recipes

References

Metric Conversion Guide

U.S.	Canada
1/4 teaspoon	1 mL
1/2 teaspoon	2 mL
1 teaspoon	5 mL
1 tablespoon	15 mL
1/4 cup	50 mL
1/3 cup	75 mL
1/2 cup	125 mL
2/3 cup	150 mL
3/4 cup	175 mL
1 cup	250 mL
1 quart	1 liter
1 ounce	30 grams
2 ounces	55 grams
4 ounces	85 grams
1/2 pound	225 grams
1 pound	455 grams

Fahrenheit	Celsius
325 degrees	160 degrees
350 degrees	180 degrees
375 degrees	190 degrees
400 degrees	200 degrees
425 degrees	220 degrees

Kitchen Safety

1. Make sure your hair and clothes will not be in the way while you are cooking.

2. Keep a fire extinguisher in the kitchen. Never put water on a grease fire.

3. Wash your hands with soap before you start to cook. Wash your hands with soap again after you handle meat or poultry.

4. Ask an adult for help with sharp knives, the stove, the oven, and all electrical appliances.

5. Turn handles of pots and pans to the middle of the stove. A person walking by could run into handles that stick out toward the room.

6. Use dry pot holders to take dishes out of the oven.

7. Wash all fruits and vegetables.

8. Always use a clean cutting board. Wash the cutting board thoroughly after cutting meat or poultry.

9. Wipe up spills immediately.

10. Store leftovers properly. Do not leave leftovers out at room temperature for more than two hours.

Cooking Equipment

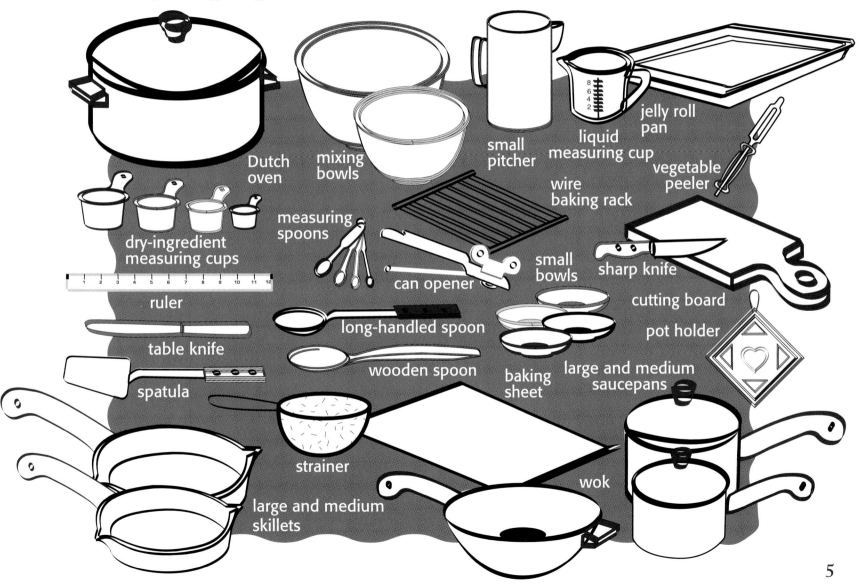

Dutch oven

mixing bowls

small pitcher

liquid measuring cup

jelly roll pan

vegetable peeler

wire baking rack

dry-ingredient measuring cups

measuring spoons

can opener

small bowls

sharp knife

cutting board

ruler

table knife

long-handled spoon

wooden spoon

baking sheet

large and medium saucepans

pot holder

spatula

strainer

large and medium skillets

wok

Discovering Gold

The California Gold Rush began quietly in 1848, near what is now the small town of Coloma, California. James Marshall, a carpenter, was overseeing the construction of a mill. One day in January, Marshall noticed a glittering rock in a ditch near the stream of the mill. After showing it to other workers, he took the nugget to John Sutter, the mill owner. The two men identified the shiny nugget as gold.

Sutter and Marshall tried to keep the discovery a secret, but it was impossible. Workers at Sutter's Mill immediately started panning for gold and never finished building the mill. Before long, word of the gold find spread to towns throughout California, to the United States, and around the world.

Californians by the thousands rushed into the foothills of the Sierra Nevada mountains to search for gold. Many of these gold seekers arrived in San Francisco carrying pouches of gold dust, flakes, and nuggets. After seeing these finds, many people left the city in search of gold. Even the soldiers who were supposed to defend San Francisco left their posts and headed for the gold mines.

Sam Brannan, an owner of a San Francisco newspaper, decided to sell mining supplies to

President James Polk announced the discovery of gold in California just a few months after Marshall found the nugget near Sutter's Mill.

Seeing the Elephant

Many people who traveled west said that they had "seen the elephant" during their journey. This expression meant that they had seen the worst of times and lived through them. The expression came from a humorous story about a farmer who wanted to see a circus elephant. He loaded his vegetables and eggs into his wagon and headed to town, hoping to catch a glimpse of the elephant while he went about his work.

As he turned a corner in town, he saw the elephant outside the circus tent. But the sight of the elephant frightened his horses. They kicked and overturned the wagon, throwing the farmer to the ground. Although he came home without any money, without a wagon, and with a broken nose and arm, he told his wife, "Never mind, I have seen the elephant."

gold prospectors for extra money. To attract new prospectors, he began printing articles about gold discoveries in his newspaper. Many people thought they could find their fortunes in the hills of California.

By 1849, the incredible stories about gold in California had stirred up excitement in Europe, Mexico, and South America. People from all over the world were reading stories about gold diggers striking it rich. People heard that gold lined the streams of California. The rush to grab a piece of the fortune began. Gold seekers knew that the sooner they reached California, the better chance they had at striking it rich. This widespread excitement to hurry to California became known as the California Gold Rush of 1849. People who made their way to California were referred to as forty-niners, prospectors, overlanders, and argonauts. All were adventurers in search of riches.

In 1849, more than 80,000 gold seekers headed for California. Many of these early prospectors were single, young men. U.S. prospectors chose between traveling an overland route and traveling by sea. Both routes averaged about 5 months, although the sea routes sometimes took longer.

For forty-niners who lived along the east coast, traveling by ship seemed like the fastest way to get to California. Unlike those traveling overland, these travelers did not need to wait until the spring thaw. Sea travelers either sailed around Cape Horn at the southern tip of South America or they sailed to Panama, crossed overland on horseback, and waited for passage on a ship to San Francisco.

Ships enroute to California were well supplied with food. They carried salt pork, beef, ham, dried beans, potatoes, rice, sweet potatoes, and tea. Travelers' meals often included fish such as salmon, sardines, bass, and cod. Passengers ate lobscouse, a hash made of salted meat, potatoes, and sea biscuits or hard bread softened with water. To flavor bad-tasting water, ship cooks made a beverage called switchel, by adding molasses, vinegar, and spices.

Since the ocean rocked ships, tables had spikes in them to hold the dishes steady. During storms, eating was almost impossible. The rocking motion of the ship sent cups and silverware crashing to the floor.

Forty-niners who traveled to Panama sometimes waited in Panama City for months before they could board a ship to San Francisco. Ships did not regularly

Gold seekers who traveled to California by ship were called argonauts. The name is from a Greek myth about a hero named Jason who sailed the ship Argo in search of the Golden Fleece.

stop at Panama City. Some
travelers feasted on tropical fruits
during their stay.

Ships sailing from Panama
generally served large or even lavish
meals. The ships' crews could afford
these meals because few forty-niners
chose to travel the Panama route, and the
voyage was not long.

Traveling by sea was expensive, and many
gold seekers chose to travel by land instead. These
forty-niners, sometimes called overlanders, packed
covered wagons with food and supplies and headed for
the California Trail. The California Trail started from
towns in Missouri, stretched westward across the plains,
and wound through the Rocky Mountains. Overlanders
formed wagon trains. These groups averaged 15 to 25
wagons that traveled together. Wagon train members
helped each other during the journey.

Overlanders packed foods that would not spoil
quickly. They loaded wagons with barrels
of flour, sacks of dried beans, rice, and
bacon. They also brought along dried
fruit, mostly apples, coffee, and molasses.
At the end of the day, overlanders chose
a spot to camp and built a fire over which
to cook the evening meal.

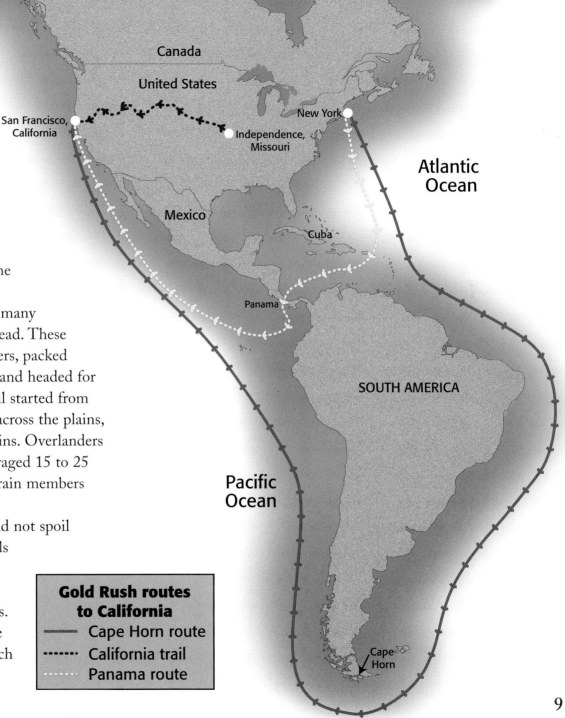

**Gold Rush routes
to California**
— Cape Horn route
······· California trail
······· Panama route

9

Switchel

Switchel was a cold beverage that farmers drank during harvest time to quench their thirst and give them an energy boost. Gold seekers often found that water aboard ships or along the California trail tasted bad. They made switchel to make muddy, germ-filled water taste a little better.

Ingredients
½ cup light brown sugar
½ cup white wine vinegar
¼ cup light molasses
1 teaspoon ground ginger
2 cups cold water

Equipment
dry-ingredient measuring cups
liquid measuring cup
measuring spoons
small pitcher
long-handled spoon

1. Combine ½ cup light brown sugar, ½ cup white wine vinegar, ¼ cup light molasses, and 1 teaspoon ground ginger in pitcher.
2. Add 2 cups cold water. Stir well with long-handled spoon.
3. Refrigerate switchel and serve cold.

Makes 6 servings

Outdoor cooking was a challenge for those traveling across the prairie. With few trees on the prairie, finding fuel for the fire was difficult. Overlanders gathered buffalo chips to fuel their fires. Strong winds blew dust into cooking pots and food. On rainy days, fires did not stay lit. Overlanders sat inside the wagon and ate leftover beans, dried fruit, and hard bread.

Overlanders cooked outdoors over an open fire. The most widely used cooking pot was the Dutch oven. This heavy, cast-iron pot could be used for baking and roasting.

Sea Biscuits

Gold seekers who sailed to California ate sea biscuits, a very hard cracker. Sea biscuits did not spoil as quickly as bread or crumble like regular crackers. Overlanders also brought hard crackers, which they called hardtack.

Ingredients
1 tablespoon butter or margarine
  for greasing
4 cups all-purpose flour
1 tablespoon salt
1 1/2 cups water

Equipment
paper towel or napkin
baking sheet
large bowl
dry-ingredient measuring cups
measuring spoons
liquid measuring cup
wooden spoon

medium bowl
table knife
ruler
fork
pot holders
metal spatula

1. Heat oven to 325°F. Use a paper towel or napkin dabbed with 1 tablespoon butter or margarine to lightly grease baking sheet.
2. In large bowl, combine 4 cups flour and 1 tablespoon salt. With wooden spoon, slowly stir in 1 1/2 cups water.
3. Turn dough out onto a lightly floured surface. Knead the dough by pushing it with the heels of your palm, fold it, and repeat. Knead for 7 to 10 minutes until dough is smooth. Add flour if dough sticks to your hand.
4. Place dough on baking sheet. Cover with medium bowl and let rest for 10 minutes.
5. Press the dough into a 1/2-inch (1.3-centimeter) thickness, making a large rectangle. Using knife and ruler, lightly mark lines into dough to divide it into 3-inch by 3-inch (7.6-centimeter by 7.6-centimeter) squares.
6. Prick the dough all over with a fork, making the holes go all the way to the bottom of the pan.
7. Bake 1 hour or until lightly browned.
8. Cool on baking sheet. Remove from pan with spatula.
9. Biscuits can be broken along score lines.

Warning: Do not eat sea biscuits without first dipping them into milk or hot chocolate. Sea biscuits may break your teeth if you eat them dry.

Makes 9 biscuits

Staking a Claim

After they reached California, forty-niners trekked to gold camps at the foothills of the Sierra Nevada Mountain Range. When new prospectors arrived at mining camps, they had to "stake" a claim. A miner could claim 10 to 50 square feet (1 to 5 square meters) of land to work. Miners spent most of their time working their claim to keep it from being jumped. Claim jumpers were thieves who took other miners' claims when they were unoccupied.

Large mining camps sprang up quickly where a gold strike had been made. Prospectors were always moving to stake a new claim near a newer gold strike. If miners continued to find gold, these camps grew into towns and cities. In some camps, the gold disappeared quickly. Miners abandoned the camps, and they became ghost towns.

Most men in mining camps cooked for themselves. They used long-handled skillets to cook over an open fire. They ate meals of dried beef, bacon, or salt pork. Some forty-niners made pots of baked beans with molasses. At times, miners hunted for raccoon, rabbit, deer, and antelope. They fished the nearby streams and rivers for salmon or trout.

Many men did not know how to cook and bake. Their breads and biscuits turned out dry and flat. Some men did not understand that water had to be added to dried beans and rice to soften them. At times, miners' meals consisted only of overcooked beans and hard bread.

Prospectors panned for gold in streams. This process was called wet digging. Those who dug up the dried up gravel bottoms of old streams were dry digging.

Forty-niners built Long Toms if they planned to mine for a long time. A Long Tom was a gently sloping, wooden chute built next to a creek. The chute was open at the top and strips of wood called riffles were nailed across the bottom. Miners shoveled dirt and gravel into the steady stream of creek water running through the Long Tom. As the creek water rushed through, dirt washed away, and the heavier gold nuggets and dust were caught by the riffles. Using Long Toms, gold seekers could sift through 1 ton (1 metric ton) or more dirt and gravel a day.

Campfire Beefsteaks

Ingredients
2 tablespoons butter or margarine
2 pounds top round or ball tip
  beef steak, ¾-inch
  (2-centimeters) thick, cut into
  6 equal pieces
1½ cups plus 3 tablespoons
  water
2 tablespoons flour
¾ teaspoon salt
½ teaspoon pepper

Equipment
large skillet
spatula
plate
aluminum foil
wooden spoon
measuring spoons
liquid measuring cup
fork

1. Melt 1 tablespoon butter in skillet.
2. Add 3 steak pieces to pan. Cook about 2½ minutes. Turn steaks over with spatula. Cook 2½ minutes more. Remove from pan to plate. Cover with foil.
3. Repeat steps 1 and 2 with remaining 3 steaks.
4. Add 1½ cups water, ¾ teaspoon salt, and ½ teaspoon pepper to pan juices. Stir well. Cook and stir 2 minutes or until hot.
5. Combine 2 tablespoons flour and 3 tablespoons water in liquid measuring cup. Mix with fork.
6. Slowly pour flour mixture into pan, stirring constantly. Bring to a boil, stirring until gravy thickens.
7. Serve steaks with gravy from pan.

Makes 6 servings

The word beefsteak comes from the practice of cooking strips of beef on a stake over an open fire. Miners often twisted a piece of iron into an s-shape and laid it on the campfire like a griddle to cook their beefsteak. Other times, they grilled their steaks in a cast-iron skillet.

Hitting the Mother Lode

Gold is found in two types of deposits—placer and lode. The California Gold Rush started with the discovery of placer deposits, or gold that was loose in gravel and sand. These deposits had washed into streams as the water eroded the gold off rocks. Gold seekers found these deposits in the sandy bottoms of streams or in the packed mud of dried-up streams. Placer mining took little skill. Prospectors called placer mines "the poor man's diggings."

Lode gold is in veins of rocks deep in mountain foothills. This type of deposit is what miners called the "mother lode." When miners hit the mother lode, they knew they had struck it rich. However, "hard rock" mining took skilled miners and was expensive to develop.

Diggings and Boomtowns

Prospectors soon learned that they may not strike it rich right away. Although some prospectors made thousands of dollars in a few months, most of the "easy pickings" had been discovered early in the Gold Rush. Eager miners who had dreamed of scooping up loose nuggets from streams found gold digging to be hard work.

Gold deposits in the creeks and rivers running from the mountain foothills down to the Sacramento Valley and the San Joaquin Valley lay hidden in rugged country. Prospectors had to scramble down steep trails to get to rivers and streams. They often stood knee deep in ice-cold water all day while the sun burned their backs and arms. Most miners found an average of $3 worth of gold a day.

Many forty-niners slept in tents in mining camps called diggings. Some of the diggings had a cook tent and a cook. But many miners had to find their own food. If prospectors ran out of food, they walked to the nearest large camp to find something to eat. While some diggings had limited food supplies, others had plenty. Hungry forty-niners hoped to buy food from other miners.

Before long, towns near the diggings opened boarding houses and hotels. Many prospectors chose to rent a room, especially during winter months when mountain weather was too cold for mining. Towns grew so quickly that they became known as boomtowns.

Even miners who could not afford to rent a room in town often went to restaurants for a warm and filling meal. Restaurants served steak, ham, salmon, biscuits and gravy, rice pudding, and fruit pies. The El Dorado, a hotel restaurant in Placerville, California, featured a menu of Mexican beef, baked beans, baked potatoes, codfish balls, grizzly bear roast, rabbit, and 18-carat hash.

Miners did not build permanent homes in the diggings. Many prospectors lived out of tents or crude shacks until they moved on to the next mining site.

18-Carat Hash

Ingredients	Equipment
2 medium potatoes	vegetable
water	peeler
1 12-ounce can corned beef	large
1 small onion	saucepan
1 tablespoon butter or	cutting board
margarine	sharp knife
¼ teaspoon salt	measuring spoons
¼ teaspoon pepper	medium skillet
dill pickles or poached eggs	wide spatula

1. With vegetable peeler, remove skin from 2 potatoes. Place potatoes in large saucepan and cover with water.
2. Place saucepan on stove and bring water to a boil. Turn heat to simmer and cook potatoes for 20 minutes or until potatoes can be easily pierced with a knife tip.
3. Remove potatoes from water and set them aside to cool.
4. Chop corned beef into ¼-inch (.6-centimeter) pieces.
5. Peel and chop 1 onion into very small pieces.
6. Chop potatoes into ¼-inch (.6-centimeter) pieces.
7. Place skillet on stove over medium heat. Melt 1 tablespoon butter or margarine in skillet.
8. Add chopped corned beef, potatoes, onion, ¼ teaspoon salt, and ¼ teaspoon pepper to skillet. Mix well.
9. Pat hash down into an even layer with a spatula.
10. Cook, uncovered, without stirring, 12 minutes or until a brown crust forms on the bottom. With spatula, turn hash over and cook 10 minutes more.
11. Serve hash with dill pickles or poached eggs.

Makes 6 servings

Other Ways to Strike It Rich

Mining was not the only way to make money during the California Gold Rush. Many people abandoned the gold mines and decided to sell food and supplies to the miners. They built stores or set up tents near the diggings to sell their goods to the prospectors. Those who provided the forty-niners with tools, groceries, building supplies, and newspapers could make a small fortune by charging high prices for necessary items.

Storekeepers kept supplies of cooking utensils, clothing, boots, and shovels. They stocked their shelves with smoked halibut, canned oysters, eggs, spices, and potatoes. Some storeowners served plates of pork and beans or flapjacks to hungry forty-niners. Storekeepers sometimes rented out a portion of the floor to a miner who was looking for a place to sleep.

Some families traveled to California in search of gold. The women sometimes set up laundries or bakeries in mining camps. Miners were willing to pay high prices for a clean shirt or a loaf of fresh-baked bread.

The laundry business boomed in mining communities. In the early months of the gold rush, launderers charged up to $20 to wash and iron a dozen shirts. Some boarding houses and hotels also offered these services for an additional charge. An area of San Francisco became known as Washerwoman's Bay because it was a center for laundries.

"I have made about $18,000 worth of pies . . . $11,000 [worth] I baked in one little iron skillet, a considerable portion by a campfire . . . I bake about 1,200 pies per month and clear $200." —an anonymous letter published in Merchant's Magazine and Commercial Review, 1852

This cartoon, "Pork and Beans in the Gold Diggins," was first published in 1849. The peddler on the left is selling a pan of beans for a pan of gold nuggets of equal size. Some miners made their fortunes in gold strikes, but they also paid high prices for food and supplies.

19

Blueberry-Peach Hand Pies

Ingredients

1 7-ounce package dried peaches
¾ cup water
2 tablespoons granulated sugar
1 15-ounce package refrigerated rolled pie
  crusts
2 to 3 tablespoons all-purpose flour
⅓ cup blueberry jam

Equipment

cutting board
sharp knife
medium saucepan
liquid measuring cup
dry-ingredient measuring cups
measuring spoons
fork
baking sheet
pot holders
wire baking rack

1. Coarsely chop 1 package of dried peaches.
2. Put chopped peaches in saucepan with ¾ cup water.
3. Cook until water boils. Lower heat to medium-low. Partially cover pan and continue cooking for 15 to 18 minutes until peach pieces are very soft. Remove saucepan from heat.
4. Add 2 tablespoons sugar to peach mixture. Stir well. Set mixture aside to cool.
5. Remove rolled pie crust pouches from refrigerator and let them stand at room temperature for 15 minutes.
6. Heat oven to 400°F.
7. Remove plastic wrapping from pie crusts. Sprinkle 2 to 3 tablespoons flour onto a cutting surface and unfold both pie crusts.
8. Cut each round of pie dough into four equal pieces along fold lines.
9. Place ¼ cup of the peach mixture in the center of each triangle-shaped pie dough piece. Spoon 1 teaspoon blueberry jam on top of peach mixture.
10. With clean fingers, brush the edges of the dough with water. Carefully fold over dough, making a triangle-shaped turnover. Press edges firmly to seal dough.
11. Crimp edges of turnovers with the tines of a fork. Cut a small slit in the top of each turnover with tip of knife.
12. Place turnovers on baking sheet.
13. Bake turnovers at 400°F for 25 minutes or until golden brown. Cool on a wire baking rack.

Makes 8 turnovers

Women who traveled to California learned that they could make a steady income by operating bakeries or by keeping a garden. Miners paid high prices for fresh-baked bread and pies. They were eager for a tasty meal with soft bread after months of eating beans and stale bread. Grocers and restaurant owners offered fresh vegetables and fruits for a high price. For a short time, markets in town charged up to $2.50 for a piece of fresh fruit.

Chocolate in the Diggings

Domingo Ghiradelli, a candy maker from Lima, Peru, exported chocolate to the growing city of San Francisco before the discovery of gold at Sutter's Mill. When he heard news of the gold rush, he too made his way to California. Ghiradelli was not successful in mining for gold. He opened a store and stocked hard-to-find luxuries such as chocolate candies. The Ghiradelli Chocolate Company still exists in San Francisco today.

Mule trains traveled from camp to camp delivering supplies to miners. Suppliers strapped sacks of food and layers of clothing on the mules' backs.

21

Going on a Bust

When forty-niners struck gold, they liked to travel to cities such as Sacramento and San Francisco to spend some of their gold dust. They dined in fancy restaurants, bought new clothes, and went to theaters and saloons. Miners called these outings "going on a bust." Eating oysters was considered a part of a wealthy lifestyle. Many miners ordered oysters to show how successful they had been.

San Francisco became known as a city of great glamour. San Francisco grew quickly as miners spent great amounts of gold celebrating their strikes and investing in land and businesses. Built along a bay, San Francisco became a major port for foreign suppliers selling merchandise. Many foreigners set up permanent shops and restaurants in San Francisco.

Ships filled with food flooded the San Francisco ports to sell to lucky miners. The city received so much food that much of it rotted before it could be sold. The surplus of food caused prices to drop. But food prices rose again after shopkeepers sold the excess food.

Lucky forty-niners ordered French champagne and dined on oysters, elk, and pastries. They ordered dishes such as turtle soup, salmon and trout with anchovy sauce, beef with mushroom sauce, veal cutlets, and lobster.

Hangtown Fry

Ingredients

½ pound bacon
½ cup all-purpose flour
⅛ and ½ teaspoon salt
⅛ and ¼ teaspoon pepper
1 cup yellow cornmeal or very fine
   cracker crumbs
7 eggs
12 fresh oysters*
*Substitute a well-drained
  8-ounce (.28-gram) can of oysters, if
  desired.

Equipment

sharp knife
cutting board
4 small bowls
medium skillet
spatula
jellyroll pan, 15½ inches by
   10½ inches (39 centimeters by
   26 centimeters)
paper towels
measuring spoons
fork
clean coffee can or other container

1. Slice bacon crosswise into ½-inch (1.3 centimeter) pieces.
2. Measure ½ cup flour into small bowl. Add ⅛ teaspoon salt and ⅛ teaspoon pepper and mix well.
3. Measure 1 cup cornmeal into another small bowl.
4. Break 1 egg into a small bowl. Lightly beat egg with fork.
5. Line jellyroll pan with paper towels. Set aside.
6. Cook bacon pieces in skillet over medium-high heat until crisp. Remove pieces from pan with spatula and drain on one side of the paper towel-lined jellyroll pan.
7. Dip each oyster into the seasoned flour mixture, then into the beaten egg, then into the cornmeal. Set in jellyroll pan opposite cooked bacon pieces.
8. Break 6 eggs into clean bowl. Add ½ teaspoon salt and ¼ teaspoon pepper. Beat lightly with fork.
9. Pour cooled bacon fat into a clean coffee can or other container. Measure 2 tablespoons bacon fat back into skillet. Heat over medium heat. Add oysters and cook 3 minutes or until golden brown. Remove from skillet. Save on a serving plate.
10. Add 6 beaten eggs to skillet. Cook, stirring gently occasionally, until set.
11. Serve eggs with oysters. Sprinkle bacon over the top.

Makes 6 servings

A Melting Pot of Gold Seekers

The California Gold Rush attracted an amazing number of people from all over the world. Most gold seekers were from the United States. But thousands came from Mexico, Peru, Chile, England, Ireland, France, Germany, Italy, Spain, Russia, Canada, and China.

People in China were suffering from recent crop failures. When news of the gold rush reached the country, many Chinese sailed to California. They called California *Gum Shan*, or Gold Mountain. Many Chinese people opened restaurants and laundries in San Francisco. Others remained in the diggings until they found gold and then returned to China.

Most gold-seekers were single men. But some women traveled to the diggings alone, and many others accompanied their husbands to California.

In 1849, about 40,000 people from all over the world came to California's gold mines. By the 1870s and 1880s, only a few lone prospectors and big mining companies were still trying to dig for gold in California's hills.

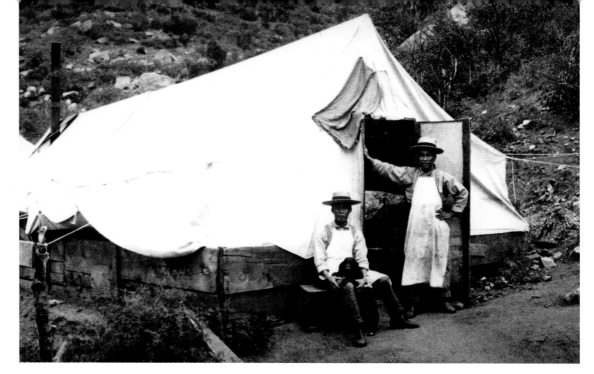

In 1848, a year before the gold rush, only a few Chinese residents made their homes in California. By 1852, about 20,000 Chinese people were living in the state. Many Chinese immigrants opened cook tents in the diggings or restaurants in nearby towns.

Chinese restaurants featured meals of won ton soup, chop suey, egg foo young, and stir fried dishes of beef, fish, or chicken and vegetables. They also introduced new foods such as bamboo shoots, stewed seaweed, shark fins, and scorpions' eggs. Chinese restaurants were popular stops for miners because the food was less expensive than it was at other restaurants.

African Americans also ventured to California. A few African Americans were slaves who accompanied their owners. Others were free blacks from the northeastern states. Many Southern gold seekers had their slaves do the hard work of mining.

Many Mexicans drove mule trains loaded with supplies to mining camps. Some miners adopted the simple Mexican recipe of refried beans. They also learned to make flour tortillas on a flapjack skillet. Other Mexicans opened restaurants where they served enchiladas and venison seasoned with chili peppers.

Prospectors forced some American Indians off their land. Some American Indians staked claims and mined for gold, while others traded and sold dried salmon, berries, and greens to forty-niners.

Many miners from the eastern United States did not treat foreigners or those of other nationalities fairly. Even though many Mexicans were skilled miners, eastern miners often drove them out of the diggings. Many eastern prospectors disliked Chinese miners because they were willing to work for less profit than eastern miners.

Chop Suey

Ingredients

½ pound partially frozen boneless pork loin roast or tenderloin
1 medium onion
3 stalks celery or bok choy (Chinese cabbage)
1 small red bell pepper
1 cup fresh bean sprouts
1 8-ounce can sliced bamboo shoots

1 8-ounce can sliced water chestnuts
½ cup chicken broth
3 tablespoons soy sauce
1 teaspoon cornstarch
2 tablespoons vegetable oil
1 teaspoon finely chopped fresh ginger root (from jar)
5 to 6 cups hot cooked rice

Equipment

cutting board
sharp knife
strainer
measuring spoons
large liquid measuring cup
Dutch oven or wok
wooden spoon
small plate or bowl

---

1. Cut pork into long, thin strips. Set aside.
2. Peel onion. Cut in half and then into thin slices.
3. Cut 3 stalks celery or bok choy in diagonal slices.
4. Cut 1 red bell pepper in half. Remove stem and seeds. Cut pepper into strips.
5. Rinse 1 cup bean sprouts in strainer. Drain cans of bamboo shoots and water chestnuts in strainer.
6. In large liquid measuring cup, combine ½ cup chicken broth, 3 tablespoons soy sauce, and 1 teaspoon cornstarch.
7. Heat 2 tablespoons oil in Dutch oven or wok. Add pork strips and ginger. Cook and stir for 2 minutes until meat is no longer pink. Remove ingredients and place on plate.
8. Add onion, celery or bok choy, bell pepper, and bean sprouts to Dutch oven or wok. Cook for 4 minutes, stirring constantly.
9. Stir broth mixture and pour it into the Dutch oven or wok. Add bamboo shoots and water chestnuts.
10. Bring mixture to boiling. Cook and stir until sauce is thickened. Add pork to other ingredients. Stir well. Serve hot over rice.

Makes 6 servings

The Golden State

The discovery of gold in California had long-lasting effects. The Gold Rush drew thousands of people to the diggings. This flood of people finished opening the West. The flow of goods and services to San Francisco and the surrounding area allowed towns and cities to grow quickly. By 1850, just two years after the discovery of gold, California had drawn enough people to become a state.

The energy and spirit of the forty-niners made a lasting impression on California. Some people made fortunes during the Gold Rush. They invested in businesses and built homes in California to help settle the state. Other prospectors worked for mining companies or became part of the growing cattle ranch business.

Chinese miners who came to California during the Gold Rush also helped bring steady settlement to the west. Many Chinese workers joined crews building the transcontinental railroad. This railroad ran from Omaha, Nebraska, to Sacramento, California. Trains traveled on railroads from the east to Omaha. From Omaha, emigrants could ride the train to the West Coast.

By the mid-1850s, many of California's streams and mountain foothills had been stripped of gold. Gold hidden deep within rock required expensive equipment to mine. New discoveries of gold led to rushes in Colorado, Idaho, and Alaska. In California, agriculture overtook mining as the main industry.

The wealth and growth in population that the Gold Rush brought encouraged more people to head west. Emigrants continued to travel from the east to build farms and businesses in California. The Gold Rush had opened the western frontier to families, businessmen, and overlanders eager to find a better life.

Boomtowns quickly sprang up near California mines. This photo of Nevada City in 1852 represents a typical boomtown.

Colache

After the gold rush, agriculture flourished in California's Central Valley. California still produces many of the fresh fruits and vegetables eaten in the United States.

Ingredients
2 small zucchinis
¼ pound fresh green beans
2 medium tomatoes
1 small onion
1 8-ounce can whole kernel corn
1 4-ounce can chopped green
  chiles
2 tablespoons olive oil
¼ teaspoon salt

Equipment
cutting board
sharp knife
can opener
strainer
Dutch oven
wooden spoon
measuring spoons

1. Wash zucchinis, green beans, and tomatoes.
2. Trim ends and cut zucchinis and green beans into ½-inch (1.3-centimeter) pieces.
3. Cut out stem and chop tomatoes.
4. Peel skin from onion and chop into small pieces.
5. Drain cans of corn and chiles in strainer.
6. Heat 2 tablespoons oil in Dutch oven over medium-high heat.
7. Add onion and green beans to Dutch oven. Cook and stir for 3 minutes.
8. Add zucchini and tomato to Dutch oven. Lower heat to medium and cover pan. Cook 8 minutes.
9. Add corn and chiles to skillet. Cook and stir for 1 to 2 minutes or until mixture is hot and all the vegetables are tender. Season with ¼ teaspoon salt.

Makes 6 servings

29

Words to Know

argonaut (AR-guh-nawt)—an adventurer on a quest

buffalo chips (BUHF-uh-loh CHIPS)—dried buffalo droppings

champagne (sham-PAYN)—a white wine that has small bubbles

emigrant (EM-uh-grehnt)—a person who travels from a home country or location to another; emigrants moved from their homes in the East to settle in the West.

immigrant (IM-uh-gruhnt)—someone who comes from abroad to live permanently in a country

impression (im-PRESH-uhn)—something that causes a strong and lasting effect

lavish (LAV-ish)—generous or more than enough

lode (LOHD)—gold deposits that are found deep within rocks

merchandise (MUR-chuhn-dys)—supplies that are sold by a store or business

overlanders (oh-vur-LAND-urs)—people who traveled west across the plains and prairies in covered wagons

placer (PLAYSS-ur)—gold deposits found in the loose gravel of streams or dried mud that have eroded from rocks

prospector (PROS-pekt-ur)—a person who explores an area for mineral deposits such as gold

provision (pruh-VIZH-uhn)—a stock of needed food and supplies

venison (VEN-uh-suhn)—the meat of a deer

To Learn More

Conlin, Joseph R. *Bacon, Beans, and Galantines: Food and Foodways on the Western Mining Frontier.* Reno: University of Nevada Press, 1986.

Ferris, Julie. *California Gold Rush: A Guide to California in the 1850s.* Sightseers. New York: Kingfisher, 1999.

Gunderson, Mary. *Oregon Trail Cooking. Exploring History through Simple Recipes.* Mankato, Minn.: Blue Earth Books, 2000.

Kalman, Bobbie D. *The Gold Rush.* Life in the Old West. New York: Crabtree Publishing, 1999.

Schanzer, Rosalyn. *Gold!.* Washington, D.C.: National Geographic Society, 1999.

Sherrow, Victoria. *Life during the Gold Rush.* The Way People Live. San Diego: Lucent Books, 1998.

Places to Write and Visit

Calaveras County Historical Society
30 North Main Street
San Andreas, CA 95249

California Historical Society
678 Mission Street
San Francisco, CA 94105

Gold Country Museum
1273 High Street
Auburn, CA 95603

Golden State Museum
California State Archives Building
1020 O Street
Sacramento, CA 95814

Marshall Gold Discovery State Historical Park
P.O. Box 265
310 Back Street
Coloma, CA 95613

Wells Fargo History Museum
1000 2nd Street
Sacramento, CA 95814

Internet Sites

California's Natural Resources
http://ceres.ca.gov/natural_resources/index.html

Gold Rush
http://www.calgoldrush.com

Gold Rush! California's Untold Stories
http://www.museumca.org/goldrush

Gold Rush Chronicles
http://comspark.com/goldminer-mall/chronicles/golddisc.htm

The Gold Rush History Alliance
http://www.timeship.com/GRHA

Women in the Gold Rush
http://www.goldrush.com/~joann/index.html

Index